BUGS

A CLOSE-UP VIEW OF THE
INSECT WORLD

BUGS

A CLOSE-UP VIEW OF THE
INSECT WORLD

By
Chris Maynard

Consultant
David Burnie

A Dorling Kindersley Book

Dorling DK Kindersley

LONDON, NEW YORK, SYDNEY, DELHI,
PARIS, MUNICH, and JOHANNESBURG

Project Editor Steve Setford
Project Art Editor Peter Radcliffe
Senior Editor Fran Jones
Senior Art Editor Marcus James
Category Publisher Jayne Parsons
Managing Art Editor Jacquie Gulliver
US Editors Gary Werner and Margaret Parrish
Picture Researcher Marie Osborn
Production Erica Rosen
DTP Designers Matthew Ibbotson and Louise Paddick

First American Edition, 2001

01 02 03 04 05 10 9 8 7 6 5 4 3 2 1

Published in the United States by
DK Publishing, Inc.
95 Madison Avenue
New York, New York 10016

A Cataloging-in-Publication record for this title is available from the Library of Congress.

ISBN 0-7894-7970-2 (pb)
ISBN 0-7894-7969-9 (hc)
Reproduced by Colourscan, Singapore
Printed and bound by L.E.G.O., Italy

See our complete catalog at
www.dk.com

CONTENTS

INTRODUCTION

Insects, or "bugs" as we like to call them, are the most successful animals on Earth. They've been scuttling around since before the first dinosaurs, and can now be found everywhere from scorching-hot deserts to icy-cold lakes. But insects are very different from us – as different as any alien you've ever seen in the movies or on television.

To start with, insects don't have a backbone. They also have their skeletons on the outside of their bodies and their flesh on the inside. They don't have lungs, but breathe through holes in their sides called spiracles. What's more, they can taste with their feet and smell with their feelers. Some can even hear through ears on their knees. And so the list goes on...
 There are also far more of them than there are of us. Some scientists think that there

MOST INSECTS, INCLUDING THIS LOCUST, HAVE WINGS TO HELP THEM GET AROUND.

may be up to 10 quintillion (10,000,000,000,000,000,000) insects alive at any one time. That's about 1.6 billion insects for every person in the world! Since there's so many of them, perhaps the Earth ought to be renamed "Planet Insect?"

Believe it or not, insects have a tremendous effect on our daily lives. Health experts estimate that one in six people in the world today suffers from an illness transmitted by insects. On the other hand, insects perform such a valuable job in pollinating plants that many of the world's plant species – upon which we rely so much for food – would disappear without them. So, you see, there are plenty of good reasons for learning about these curious creatures.

For those who want to explore the subject in more detail, there are black "Log On" boxes that appear throughout the book. These will direct you to some exciting websites where you can find out even more. Welcome to the truly mind-boggling, totally fascinating world of insects!

WHAT ARE BUGS?

We may think we know what bugs are. But most of us find it tricky to say exactly what it is that makes a bug a bug. For a start, bugs are tiny animals that crawl. True. And creep. Correct. And fly into your hair. Not bad. And have zillions of tiny legs. Wrong!

Although many creepy crawlies look like bugs, real bugs only ever have six legs. Anything else is a fake, or a bug that's lost a leg in an accident.

Bugs or insects

When people use the word "bugs," they usually mean "insects." But strictly speaking "bugs" means something very different to insect scientists (or entomologists, to give them their proper title). This is because among the 30 or so main groups of insects – cockroaches, beetles, ants, flies, and so on – there is a group called "bugs." It has the scientific name of Hemiptera, but all the insects in this group are properly called "true bugs."

SIX STRONG, JOINTED LEGS, TWO FEELERS, AND A SET OF WINGS PROVE THAT THIS COLORFUL ASSASSIN BUG IS A GENUINE INSECT.

WEIRD WORLD
IN 1758, SWEDISH NATURALIST CAROLUS LINNAEUS PUBLISHED DESCRIPTIONS OF 654 SPECIES OF BEETLE. TODAY, WE KNOW OF 370,000 BEETLE SPECIES – AND THE NUMBER'S STILL RISING!

True bugs, such as aphids or stinkbugs, have no teeth or mouths that chew. Instead, they have a beak in the shape of a straw with a needlelike point. That doesn't mean they sit around sipping soft drinks all day. What they do is use their beaks to punch holes in things and suck out the juices inside. The "things" they sip from may be plants or animals – even humans if the bugs happen to be bloodthirsty bedbugs.

The leg test

The only surefire way to tell an insect from another animal is to count its legs. But first you must persuade it to keep still long enough for you to count. When you're carrying out your leg tests, remember that all insects have six legs. Always!

Many people think that spiders are insects – think again. Check the legs and you'll find that spiders have eight of them, and that proves they aren't insects. Nor are woodlice with 14. Nor are centipedes, which have a minimum of 30 legs (but not 100, as the name

JUST LIKE THIS DAMSELFLY, ALL INSECTS HAVE THREE-PART BODIES WITH A HEAD, A THORAX (THE MIDDLE PART), AND AN ABDOMEN (THE REAR PART).

implies). The same goes for worms and slugs, which have no legs at all.

Introducing arthropods

The reason why it's so easy to mix up insects and other creeping creatures is because they're all distant cousins. Insects are arthropods. (The "pod" part means we're still talking about legs.) Arthropods all have jointed legs, just as our own legs have knees and ankles. They also have a hard outer skeleton that protects the vital parts inside it. This is known as the exoskeleton. Apart from insects, arthropods include crabs and prawns, spiders, mites, and millipedes.

Luckily, insects differ from other arthropods in a few really important ways. First, they have a body with three parts – a head, a thorax (the middle part, to which the legs are attached), and an abdomen (the rear part, which contains the heart, digestive system, and sexual organs). Second, they have a single pair of antennae, or feelers, on their heads. Finally, most insects (but not all) have one or two pairs of wings. Ants and termites, which are insects, don't usually have wings. Most other insects do, and some, such as dragonflies and damselflies, can zip along as fast as birds.

The secret of their success

If you get really close to an insect – and remember they're wild animals that might be in the mood to bite you – ponder this question. What is it about insects that makes them the most successful animals ever to have lived on Earth?

THE PRAYING MANTIS USES ITS POWERFUL MOUTHPARTS LIKE A BUZZ SAW TO TEAR PREY TO SHREDS.

The big edge insects have over other animals is their smallness. Most people imagine that your chances in the wild improve if you're big. But bugs hit the big time by being small. The majority of insects are under 1 in (25 mm) long.

Among the smallest even this would seem gigantic. In fact, insects such as fleas, lice, thrips,

BULLDOG ANTS OF AUSTRALIA HAVE LONG, SHARP JAWS LINED WITH SPINES.

and bristletails are so tiny that it's easy to miss them altogether if you blink.

A RAIDING PARTY OF ANTS
DRAGS AN UNLUCKY VICTIM
BACK TO THE ANT COLONY
FOR A BITE TO EAT!

in the tiniest nooks or crannies. Fleas lead a warm and cosy life between the hairs of a cat's fur, and not even the most determined scratching bothers them much. Other insects, like leaf miners and some thrips, live snugly between the paper-thick top and bottom layers of leaves. Beetles of all kinds burrow under tree bark and into the wood, where nobody ever disturbs them.

The other really clever thing about being small is that it takes a lot less than a hamburger to feed you. Insects thrive on the tiniest scraps of food. Even in hard times, when other animals struggle to find food, there's always likely to be enough to keep insects happy.

The real minis, like feather-winged beetles, are not much larger than the dot at the end of this sentence. They live happily, if disgustingly, in rotting animal dung, where they snack away on fungus spores. It takes a lot of concentration, and a strong nose, even to find one.

Smallest of all are the fairy flies. They are about a quarter of the size of a pinhead, but they still get along very nicely, thank you, by laying their eggs in the eggs of other insects.

Small is smart

Being small means that insects can shelter

WEIRD WORLD

THE BIGGEST INSECTS THE WORLD HAS EVER SEEN WERE DRAGONFLIES THAT LIVED IN SWAMPS ABOUT 300 MILLION YEARS AGO. FOSSILS OF THESE DRAGONFLIES SHOW THAT THEY HAD WINGSPANS OF UP TO 29.5 IN (75 CM).

Small is risky

The most obvious disadvantage of being small is that most other things can squash you flat. As a car windshield on a summer night shows, millions of insects get flattened every day simply by being in the wrong place at the wrong time. Likewise, if you are an insect minding your own business on a leaf and you're the size of a match head, a single drop of rain falling on you will feel like being hit by a flying chimney.

The big boys

A few bugs, though not many, have found it easier to get by in

THE ATLAS MOTHS OF SOUTHEAST ASIA AND INDIA ARE FLYING GIANTS, WITH A WING AREA GREATER THAN ANY OTHER SPECIES OF INSECT.

year round. The heaviest insect is Africa's Goliath beetle. Fully grown, it may weigh 3.5 oz (100 g) – as much as a cup of sugar. The Hercules beetle is another huge insect, sometimes growing up to 7.5 in (19 cm) long. But because half of its length consists of a massive horn, it actually weighs less than the Goliath. The longest insect

the world by growing big. They all live in the tropics, where conditions are kinder to insects and where there is plenty of food all

THE GOLIATH BEETLE IS THE MONSTER OF THE INSECT WORLD. IT WOULD COVER YOUR HAND IF IT LANDED ON IT. THIS BEETLE FEEDS ON FRUIT HIGH UP IN THE TREES.

numbers. This means not only the number of different types, or species, of insect, but also the number of individual insects. Entomologists know of more than a million different insect species, and they discover about 8,000 new ones every year. They suspect there may be another four million or so species awaiting discovery. In comparison, there are less than 10,000

EIGHT OUT OF 10 OF ALL ANIMAL SPECIES ARE INSECTS

of all is the giant stick insect of Indonesia. It can reach 12 in (30 cm), the length of a size-10 men's shoe. Some tropical butterflies and moths also grow into giants. The wingspan of the Queen Alexandra's birdwing butterfly of Papua New Guinea is 11 in, (28 cm) – the same width as a large dinner plate.

S trength in numbers
What insects lack in size they more than make up for in sheer

species of bird in the world and not even 5,000 mammal species.

L ong-term residents
One reason why there are so many insects is that they have been around for an awfully long time. Insects showed up on Earth about 400 million years ago, way before there were mammals,

birds, or even any dinosaurs. So they have had plenty of time to find ways to colonize the planet. In fact, the only places you won't find insects are on the tops of the highest mountains, at the North and South Pole, and in the oceans.

Weird food

Another secret of insects' success is their varied diet. You name it – wood, soap, oil, paint, dung – and there's probably an insect that feeds on it. It's a clever tactic. After all, if you can eat your surroundings, you're sure to survive!

IN COLD WINTERS, LADYBUGS CLUSTER TOGETHER TO HIBERNATE. IN SUMMER, WHEN FOOD IS PLENTIFUL, HUGE LADYBUG SWARMS MAY FORM.

BUGS BY THE BILLION

I f you had a penny for every insect on Earth, you'd be the proud owner of a penny mountain so high that people could ski down it! Scientists know that there are simply too many insects to count. To get an idea of the number of insects crawling around out there, they take samples and study insects closely to see how they live and breed.

Tons of termites

Termites are easy to study because they live in colonies and build huge mounds. A large colony may be home to about seven million termites – as many as the human inhabitants of a city the size of New York, or London, England.

If you could take all the termites in the world and weigh them, and compare the result with the weight of all six billion of us human beings, you'd find that termites win convincingly by two to one. That's an awful lot of termites.

Locust swarms

Perhaps the scariest way to get an idea of insect numbers is to stand in the flight path of locusts as they swarm from the desert looking for food. Locusts are a type of large grasshopper. They live in dry areas of north Africa, the Middle East, and Australia. Mostly they are shy, drab-colored, and lead a pretty lonely life. But when the rains come, they throw some of the biggest, most colorful insect parties ever seen.

Hip hoppers

To prepare for the party, the females lay a lot more eggs than usual in the moist soil. For once, most of the eggs survive. A few weeks later, out hatches an army of young locusts that looks dressed up to go to a ball. Instead of being dull green and gray, these hip-looking hoppers have flashy orange, yellow, and black colors. They are no longer shy, and soon get together to form groups.

Groups join up to form bands, and the bands begin to merge until many square miles of desert scrub are heaving with swarms of young hoppers.

Blizzard of bugs

It doesn't take long for the locusts to eat every last leaf and blade of grass. By now they are winged adults, so they fly off to hunt for fresh food. A single square mile of countryside may have 200 million locusts moving through it. Really huge plagues can be more than 100 times bigger. The billions of

A SINGLE LOCUST EATS ITS OWN WEIGHT IN GRASS AND LEAVES EVERY DAY. A SWARM OF LOCUSTS CAN STRIP BARE A WHOLE FIELD OF GRAIN IN JUST A COUPLE OF HOURS.

LOG ON...
www.insects.org/ has stunning insect photos

A LOCUST SWARM LOOKS LIKE A BLIZZARD AS IT FILLS THE SKY. THE SWARM KEEPS GOING, FLYING AND FEEDING, UNTIL THE SUPPLY OF FRESH FOOD RUNS OUT.

locusts in them chomp through as much food in a day as it takes to feed New York City. Wherever the swarm settles, the locusts strip the land bare. In 1957, one swarm of locusts in Africa polished off 184,000 tons of grain before the outbreak died down. This was enough grain to feed a million people for a year. In 1998, a single plague of locusts kept on growing and spreading until it stretched from Iran in the Middle East to the Atlantic coast of northwest Africa.

Millions of midges

In many parts of the world, clouds of midges swirl above lakes and ponds. Midges are tiny flies – so tiny, in fact, that some people call them "no-see-ums." (Biting kinds ought to be called "boy-can you-feel-ums!") Midges are far too small to track in the air, but American entomologists

NONBITING MIDGES LIVE FOR A COUPLE OF WEEKS. THEY MATE ON THE WING IN A SWARM AND LAY THEIR EGGS IN A MASS OF STICKY JELLY ON WATER OR PLANTS.

have counted up to 50,000 midge larvae in a 3-feet (1-m) square of lake mud. In eastern Africa, by Lake Victoria, midges swarm so thickly that local people gather them in handfuls and press them into mushy cakes. These midge cakes are

swarming over garden roses. A female aphid can produce 50 babies a week. If conditions were ideal, and all the young aphids survived and had babies in turn, after just one year the Earth's surface would be 93 miles (150 km)

ONE LOCUST SWARM WAS 40 BILLION ADULTS STRONG

then baked on a fire and eaten with great delight. How many midges in a midge cake? No one knows – everybody's too busy eating to count them!

S wimming in aphids
The reason why there are so many insects is no big secret. It's because insects have babies just like beaches have grains of sand. In other words, the numbers are incredible. The champion mother of them all is the aphid. This is a small, soft-bodied insect that feeds on plant sap and can often be seen

deep in aphids. Thankfully, plenty of animals eat aphids, so we don't have to swim through a sea of them every time we leave the house.

APHIDS ARE GARDEN PESTS. LUCKILY, INSECTS SUCH AS LACEWINGS KEEP APHID NUMBERS IN CHECK – EACH LARVA CAN EAT 200 APHIDS A WEEK.

19

WHERE INSECTS LIVE

Insects are everywhere. They have colonized our planet more successfully than mammals, birds, or any other type of animal. What's more, they're not averse to sharing our homes with us. And brace yourself for some shocking news, because they also like to take up residence on our bodies – and that's just a bit too close for comfort!

Lice on your head

There's an insect the size of a sesame seed that spends its whole life on humans – the head louse. It latches onto a strand of human hair with its six strong legs and snuggles low, close to the scalp where it's warm and dark. When it gets hungry it crawls down, pokes a hole in the skin, and takes a sip of blood. The only time you'll notice it is when you scratch because itchy louse saliva has dribbled into your

A HEAD LOUSE CLINGS TIGHTLY TO A SHAFT OF HAIR. THE OVAL BLOB IS AN EGG.

A HUNGRY BEDBUG CAN FILL UP
WITH SIX TIMES ITS OWN WEIGHT
IN BLOOD DURING A MEAL.

skin. The little stowaway moved onto your head when your hair brushed against the hair of someone who had lice.

Fleas on your pets

Do you have a cat or a dog? If you do, you may also have pets that you didn't know you had. Pets called fleas. And they too suck blood. The good news is that fleas don't live on people the way lice do. They simply come, bite, and go. But they never go far away. They lie patiently in wait in bedding, carpets, and rugs until a meal comes along. Then they pop out and spring onto a passing victim, which could be a cat, a dog, or you – they're not fussy. A hungry flea will bite several times a minute. You'll know your new pet has landed when your skin reacts to the flea bites.

Bugs in the bed

Suppose you got rid of every louse on your head and every flea in your carpets. Time to flop on your bed with a sigh of relief. Well don't! In the cracks of beds and in old mattress seams live other bloodsuckers called bedbugs. They emerge at night and ease their sharp beaks into exposed areas of your skin. Then they take a long, thirst-quenching drink. Ten minutes later, and full to bursting, they drop off and stagger away.

WEIRD WORLD

FIREBRATS ARE SMALL, WINGLESS INSECTS KNOWN FOR THEIR ABILITY TO TOUGH IT OUT IN VERY HOT, DRY PLACES. THEY ARE OFTEN FOUND LIVING IN CRACKS BEHIND FIREPLACES OR IN BAKERS' OVENS.

Roaches in the kitchen

Bitten to pieces, you may take refuge in the kitchen. Guess what? All over the world people share their homes, especially their kitchens, with greasy cockroaches. Roaches feed on scraps of food and garbage, from dried pasta to bits of paper. These thumb-size critters can slink under sinks, squeeze through cracks no thicker than a matchstick, and scuttle along pipes to get everywhere. They don't bite or sting, but they do carry germs and reproduce so rapidly that they can take up every corner of your home.

ROACHES HAVE BEEN SEEN ON SPACECRAFT

Here, there, everywhere

Aside from living it up with humans, insects thrive in meadows, scrubland, heaths, woods, and most other habitats. The one habitat they've never really come to terms with is the ocean. A few species skate about over the surface, but apart from that the seas are insect-free. Because the majority of insects feed on plants – and most of the rest prey on these plant-eaters – insects are most plentiful in tropical rain forests, which have the most abundant plant life on Earth. One rain-forest tree can be home to about 580 insect species.

DUNG FLIES LIVE IN MEADOWS, WHERE THEY LAY THEIR EGGS IN DUNG PATS. WHEN THE YOUNG HATCH, THEY FEAST ON DUNG.

They live all over the tree,
from its underground roots
to its uppermost leaves, and
from its gnarled bark right down
into the heart of the trunk.

A dapt and prosper

Insects are so widespread
because, over millions of years,
their bodies have changed, or
adapted, to suit a whole variety
of surroundings. They are
also helped by their amazing
exoskeleton. This tough shell
is worn on the outside of the
body like a suit of armor. It's
strong. It's light. It helps to
insulate the body. And it's got
a waxy waterproof coating that
prevents the body fluids from
leaking out. Dressed in this
protective suit, they can tackle
the harshest conditions and
live in some of the world's
most inhospitable places.

I n extreme cold

In which continent is an insect
the biggest land animal of all?
The answer is Antarctica! The
winner
is a tiny,
wingless
midge, a
mere 0.5 in
(12 mm) long,
that survives
despite being
frozen stiff for
much of the year.
When the weather
warms up, the midge
thaws out and becomes active.
The only other Antarctic
insects are the lice and ticks that
live among bird feathers and seal
fur. Many insects can survive
extreme cold because they have
a kind of antifreeze in their
bodies to keep them from

23

freezing solid. It enables rock crawlers, which are cousins of crickets, to live quite happily in mountain snow with not a glove or scarf among them.

In hot and dry places
Insects are also good at living in deserts. Lots of beetles and cockroaches scuttle about in the baking desert heat, digging down into the sand if the sun is too fierce. Many desert insects never see a drop of rain in their lives. But their watertight

---

THIS DESERT BEETLE GETS THE MOISTURE IT NEEDS BY STANDING STILL AND ALLOWING DROPLETS OF WATER FROM THE EARLY MORNING MIST TO COLLECT ON ITS BODY.

skeletons prevent their bodies from losing moisture, so they rarely need to drink. The larvae of one African midge dry out completely in long droughts. Although this would kill other animals, when the rain does come the larvae are able to rehydrate, revive, and go about their business.

Under the ground
Some insects have adapted to living in the soil, where there are plenty of roots and rotting plant and animal remains to feast on. Once they take up a life of tunneling, they have no call anymore for big wings or

long legs.
That's why
mole
crickets'
wings are
tiny and
tucked out of the way on
their backs. Their short digging
legs are shaped like shovels,
and their bodies are smooth and
round. Ant-loving crickets are
wingless, small, and flat, so they
can wriggle inside an ant colony
and live there without breaking
the place apart. They wolf
down ants' eggs, food scraps
from their hosts, and fluids
produced by the ants' bodies.

In the dark

Some insects only visit caves
for food and shelter. Others
move in for good. Many
beetles and crickets love the
damp and dark there and share
it with spiders, millipedes, and
flatworms. Cave crickets have
changed a lot by living as they
do. They never chirp like other
crickets. Their eyesight is
weak, but these crickets make
up for it with hugely long
antennae and legs for smelling
and touching things. Whenever
anything moves nearby, the
crickets detect it immediately.

In many New Zealand caves,
the roof seems to twinkle with
tiny blue stars. The "stars" are
actually fungus gnat larvae that
glow with light to attract prey.
Insects flying toward the
light flutter into sticky
feeding lines lowered by
the fungus gnat larvae.
Then the larvae reel
in their prey and
eat them up.

On water

Many insects love ponds, rivers, and lakes. But they don't all swim or float. In fact, some don't even get wet. This is because insects such as water crickets and water striders are so light that they can stand on top of water. They are held up by a force called surface tension. This force pulls water molecules together and causes the surface of water to behave like a springy skin. The "skin" supports small insects so that they don't sink. They just skate over the surface as if it were ice. As they glide about, they use their front legs to catch food, the middle ones to propel them over the surface, and their back legs to steer.

Under the water

Some insects swim about or crawl along on the bottom of rivers and streams, carrying their own air bubbles with them like tiny scuba divers. Both water boatmen and diving beetles have long, hairy hind legs so they can paddle around underwater. Diving beetles eat insect larvae, snails, and worms. They are excellent swimmers and can even catch small fish and tadpoles. Water scorpions do it differently. They hang just under the surface, breathing air through a snorkel-like tube, ready to grab with their

WHEN HUNTING UNDERWATER, A GREAT DIVING BEETLE BREATHES AIR CARRIED BENEATH ITS WING CASES OR BETWEEN ITS BODY HAIRS.

A WATER BOATMAN
TRAPS BUBBLES OF AIR
ON THE UNDERSIDE OF ITS
BODY, THEN SWIMS ALONG,
JUST UNDER THE SURFACE,
LOOKING FOR PREY.

strong claws any insects they find resting on the surface.

In odd places

The most bizarre dwelling places belong to insect larvae. The larvae of the petroleum fly live in pools of crude oil, where they wriggle about waiting to devour other insects that get trapped in the sticky goo. Even more strange are scuttlefly larvae. Some have been found living in shoe

polish and paint, in dead human bodies pickled in formalin (a fluid doctors use to preserve things), and even in the lungs of living people!

Less gruesome, but still likely to put you off homemade cakes, are the beetle larvae that live in bags of flour in kitchen cabinets. But that takes us back home again, which is where we started.

CADDIS FLY LARVAE
LIVE ON THE
BOTTOM OF
PONDS, HIDING
FROM PREDATORS
IN A SILK TUBE
COVERED WITH
LEAVES, STONES,
AND SAND.

WEIRD WORLD

THE LARVAE OF CERTAIN FLIES LIKE TO BASK IN THE WATER OF HOT SPRINGS. AT 120°F (49°C), THIS IS THE "OUCH!" END OF WHAT PASSES FOR A SOAK IN A HOT BATH. MOST LIVING THINGS WOULD DIE IF HEATED TO THIS DEGREE.

ON THE MOVE

Forget superheroes! Ignore astronauts! If you really want to find out about flying, you'd better check with the experts – insects. Insects were the first animals on Earth to fly, making their maiden flights more than 300 million years ago. Insects also walk, hop, squirm, and crawl, but it's their wings that make them so special.

DRAGONFLIES CAN HOVER WELL BECAUSE ONE PAIR OF WINGS BEATS UPWARD WHILE THE OTHER BEATS DOWNWARD.

Benefits of flight

What's so great about being able to fly? Well, for a start, flying enables insects to wander a whole lot farther in search of food. It also helps them to meet a wider circle of fellow insects when looking for a mate. And if they are in danger of becoming someone's lunch, flight gives them a better chance of escape.

Insect flying aces

The Formula 1 fliers of the insect world are dragonflies. The fastest reach speeds of more than 30 mph (50 kmh) as they race up and down rivers hunting for bugs to eat. Their flight muscles are so powerful that they can even buzz in one spot like tiny helicopters or fly backward and loop the loop.

Size and wingbeats

It sounds like common sense to say that the biggest insects with the most muscles ought to

be able to flap their wings harder and faster than their puny cousins. Well, ignore common sense for once. As a rule, it turns out that the larger the bug, the slower it beats its wings as it flies. Big swallowtail butterflies fly with as few as five beats a second. Medium-size bumblebees drone among flowers at about 200 beats. Meanwhile, some tiny midges, half the size of an eyelash, can beat their wings over 1,000 times a second.

Wing arrangements

Fast fliers, such as damselflies and dragonflies, have two pairs of wings and each set flaps independently. Other insects, including moths and butterflies, have hooks that yoke their pairs of

A COCKCHAFER BEETLE HOLDS ITS
THICK WING CASES OUT OF THE WAY
TO GIVE ITS REAR WINGS ROOM TO
UNFOLD AND FLUTTER.

wings together. In flight, both sets move as one. Beetles are slightly more complicated. Although they have four wings, only the rear two are used to get airborne. The front two have developed into tough protective cases. When a beetle is on the ground, these wing cases cover the delicate flying wings behind so that they don't get damaged. When the beetle takes off, the wing cases move up and out of the way while the back pair do all the hard work. This makes beetles slow and clumsy in the air.

How to land on a ceiling

If an insect has just two wings it's sure to be a fly. In true flies, the back wings have become a pair of balancing knobs instead. These help flies to judge their speed and position in the air. What's more, they enable houseflies to pull off the great aerobatic trick of landing upside down on a ceiling – remarkable, considering that no fly can fly upside down! As it

MONARCH BUTTERFLIES ARE SERIOUS TRAVELERS. EACH YEAR THEY FLY SOUTH FROM CANADA TO CALIFORNIA AND MEXICO TO ESCAPE THE COLD. THEY COVER UP TO 80 MILES (120 KM) A DAY.

THE BIGGEST FLY IN THE WORLD IS THE SIZE OF YOUR THUMB

scoots along just below the ceiling, a fly lifts its front legs up and grips the surface above. Then it swings its body around, like a gymnast on the parallel bars, and lands four more feet neatly on the ceiling. Plunk, end of trick! Well, not quite…

Sticky feet
As well as this amazing landing ability, flies can also walk quite happily upside down. They can do this because they have sticky pads on their feet. Imagine having Velcro™ on the soles of your feet that was strong enough to take your weight. You would be able to walk anywhere – even on walls and ceilings.

Looking at legs
Insect legs, like human ones, are for walking, running, and jumping. But they seriously put us to shame. If we had legs like insects' we would have to

rewrite the book of Olympic records. Take grasshoppers and locusts, for example. They have long hind legs with huge muscles, so that when they jump they take off like a rocket. The longest leap by a locust with its wings closed is about 20 in (50 cm) – 10 times the length of its body. (How many of your own body lengths can you jump?) The secret is that, size for size, grasshopper muscles are 1,000 times stronger than human muscles.

FOR THEIR LONGEST LEAPS, GRASSHOPPERS AND LOCUSTS OPEN THEIR WINGS IN MID LEAP AND GLIDE.

even any breakfast – it can leap 100 times its own height. These great leaping powers come from rubbery pads at the base of its back legs. The pads are squeezed tightly by muscles and kept compressed until the flea needs to jump. Then they are released by a trigger mechanism and the flea is catapulted upwars with an easily heard "click."

FLEAS LIFT OFF 20 TIMES MORE QUICKLY THAN SPACE ROCKETS

High-jump specialist

Insects have got jumping down to a fine art – especially fleas. Well-trained athletes can just about leap up to their own height. In the pole vault they may get up to three times higher. That wouldn't impress a flea. Without any training – or

The mechanics of walking

Not all insects are spectacular jumpers. Walking and running are good enough for most of them. For a long time, nobody could quite figure out how an insect could walk with six legs without tripping over itself. That is, until high-speed film revealed exactly how ants move. As they walked, the ants kept three legs on the ground, and moved the other three legs forward. And it wasn't just any old three legs. It was always the front and back legs on one side and the middle leg on the other side that stayed put, while the other three legs moved. Then the two sets of legs

Muscles for bustling

Insects get the power to bustle along from muscles inside the thorax – the middle part of the body (this also contains the wing muscles in flying insects). The thorax muscles do the job of moving the legs to and fro, while tiny muscles inside the legs are used to bend the joints.

Sprint challenge

When humans, cats, or horses run fast, there is a point at which all of their legs are in the air at once. Yet no matter how fast insects travel, some of their legs always stay on the ground. Fine, you say. That's because insects don't move

swapped over. If you think about, it's not all that different from the way we walk – 50 percent of our legs stay down and 50 percent move forward!

A HUNGRY FLEA CAN LEAP 30 CM (12 IN) HIGH AND UP TO 600 TIMES AN HOUR.

GIANT WATER BUGS PADDLE WITH THEIR
REAR AND MIDDLE LEGS. THEY USE THE
FRONT PAIR TO
SEIZE PREY.

WEIRD WORLD
GYPSY MOTH CATERPILLARS
USE THE WIND TO REACH NEW
FOOD PLANTS. THEY DANGLE
FROM A TWIG ON A LINE OF SILK
UNTIL A BREEZE BLOWS THEM
AWAY AND THEY DRIFT TO A NEW
FEEDING SPOT NEARBY.

other words, if roaches were as big as humans they'd be able to run 10 times faster than we could!

very fast. Hold on! Let's do some math to check this. Human beings can run at up to 22 mph (35 kmh). That's about four body lengths a second. A running cockroach, one of the world's fastest insects, has a top speed of about 3 mph (5 kmh). This is only walking speed for us, but for roaches it amounts to 40 body lengths a second. In

All-purpose legs

Insect legs have many more uses than just walking, running, and jumping. Butterflies can use their front pair for tasting food, while bees have special brushes and baskets on their legs for gathering

A PRAYING MANTIS CATCHES VICTIMS WITH
ITS FRONT LEGS, WHICH ARE STUDDED
WITH SPINES AND HOOKS.

pollen. Grasshoppers can "sing" by rubbing their back legs against their wings to make sounds, and crickets hear using "ears" on their knees.

Legs, you'll remember, can also be used for digging, swimming, and scooting over water. Some insects have even turned their legs into hunting weapons. A praying mantis, for example, has mighty front legs that look as if it's been working out in the gym. It uses them to snatch prey and hold it in a body lock that stops the victim from struggling as it's eaten alive.

F alse legs

Caterpillars are tricky. They seem to have zillions of legs, but if you flip one over and count, all you get is six – just like every other insect. The real legs are bunched up at the front. They are used to guide leaves into the caterpillar's jaws and to help with walking. The rest of what look like legs are really muscles that stick out from the body. Each of these "prolegs" has a circle of hairs at the tip. This enables the proleg to grip surfaces as the caterpillar shuffles along.

Some caterpillars don't even bother to walk. To avoid danger, they just drop off their treetop perch on a silk safety thread!

A SWALLOWTAIL CATERPILLAR GRIPS A PLANT WITH ITS LEGS AND PROLEGS.

HOMEMAKERS

Most insects live nomadic lives, flitting from place to place. As long as they can find food, a mate, and shelter, they're content. They're not lazy, it's just that they don't need homes like we do. Some insects take the time to build nests to protect their eggs and young. Still others, called social insects, live together in colonies.

Living together

Social insects include termites, ants, and some wasps and bees. Every colony contains a queen, who lays all the eggs. All the other inhabitants of the colony are her children. Most are workers, who look after the nest, care for the young, and find food. There may also be soldier insects who defend the nest against intruders. They all live together as a one huge family.

Queen of construction

Big families need big homes, and that means lots of building. Most construction is done by the workers, using their mouthparts. But when a queen common wasp wants to start a new colony, she does all the dirty work herself, since there are no workers to help her. In the spring, the queen chews up fibers of wood and turns them into a pulp like papier-mâché. This is her building material. First she builds a short stalk, and then adds an umbrella-shaped cap. Below it she builds a comb with half a dozen cells, where she lays her first eggs. While waiting for the

A QUEEN COMMON WASP SHAPES THE WALLS OF THE NEST INTO LAYERS TO PROTECT THE EGGS WITHIN.

eggs to hatch, she builds a
series of papery shells around
the comb to keep out
the wind and rain.
When the young
wasps turn into
adult workers,
they carry on the
construction to
enlarge
the nest in
time for the next generation.
The nest grows swiftly until it's
the size of a basketball. When
complete, it may hold over
500 wasps at a time. But
hard work kills – over
spring and summer a total
of 10,000 wasps may live
there. Most live short lives
and soon die of exhaustion.

S olitary wasps and bees
Most wasps and bees live
alone, preferring their own
company to the hustle and
bustle of life in a colony.
In fact, they are such
loners that they don't even
meet the young that hatch from
their eggs. Just to show that
they care, they make nests for
their young in places such as
old spider burrows, hollow
plant stems, holes in rotting
trees, and even in snail shells.

PAPER WASPS FEED PIECES OF CHEWED-UP
CATERPILLARS TO LARVAE DEVELOPING
INSIDE THE CELLS OF THE NEST.

A MUD-DAUBER WASP BUILDS A MUD NEST ON A TREE AND LAYS A SINGLE EGG INSIDE.

Some wasps and bees are more fussy and put extra effort into nest building. A sand wasp digs a burrow in sandy ground, into which she puts a single egg and a fat caterpillar for her offspring's first meal. She plugs the entrance with sand, head-butts it firmly shut, and flies off.

Masons, potters, carpenters
Sand is just one of the many building materials used by solitary wasps and bees. Mason bees, and mud-dauber and potter wasps, create mud-pie nests out of balls of moist soil. A female mason bee scouts out a crack in a wall or an old bore-hole in wood left by a beetle. She carries mud to the site and molds it into a cell, which she lines with chewed leaves and animal hair. Then she packs the cell with pollen and nectar and lays an egg on top. The bee caps the cell with a lid of mud. When she's finished, she leaves behind a nest of half a dozen cells.

You have to like working with wood to be a good carpenter. A female carpenter bee prefers to build with timber rather than mud. To build a nest, she just

WEIRD WORLD

IN A YEAR, A HONEYBEE HIVE MAY PRODUCE UP TO 100 LB (45 KG) OF HONEY, WITH WORKERS VISITING 2–3 MILLION FLOWERS EVERY DAY. TO MAKE 2.2 LB (1 KG), THEY MAY HAVE TO COLLECT NECTAR FROM 60 MILLION FLOWERS.

chews a tunnel into wood. Then she carves out a cell with her jaws where she can lay her egg.

Honey-reared kids

Honeybees that are farmed have a much easier life. In the wild, these social insects build hives in hollow trees or in holes in cliffs. But they are more than the worker bees collect from flowers. Young bees are first fed on "royal jelly" (a nutritious saliva produced by the workers) and then on honey and pollen.

Ant architects

Ants are ingenious when it comes to nest building. Army ants, for example, have no need

HONEYBEE QUEENS USE SCENT TO CONTROL THE WORKERS

happy to make their homes in the artificial hives that are put out for them by beekeepers. A big hive may have 80,000 workers within, all ruled by a single queen. She will have to lay over 1,000 eggs a day to keep the place buzzing.

The hive itself is filled with several rows of combs. Each comb has hundreds of six-sided cells that are built of wax secreted by the worker bees' bodies. Some cells have eggs and larvae in them. Others are full of pollen and honey, which is made from a sweet liquid called nectar that

BUMBLEBEES LIVE IN SMALL COLONIES. THE QUEENS MAKE THEIR NESTS IN OLD MOUSE BURROWS OR IN CLUMPS OF TALL, THICK GRASS.

several
ant-layers
thick – very snug!

Wonderful weavers

Just as amazing are weaver ants, which make nests in trees by sewing together groups of large leaves. Teams of workers pull two leaves close to each other and hold them steady. Then smaller workers come along carrying larvae in their jaws. The larvae squirt jets of sticky silk from their heads when touched by the workers' feelers. Their handlers use the silk to "stitch" the leaf edges together.

WORKER WEAVER ANTS BUILD A TREE NEST. A SINGLE COLONY MAY INHABIT SEVERAL BALL- OR COLUMN-SHAPED NESTS.

for permanent homes, because they are always on the move. Instead, these roving insects make camp in a temporary nest formed from their own bodies! They cluster together on the forest floor and grip each other with their clawed feet. The finished nest (called a "bivouac") is like a closed bag,

Underground cities

Ants that live below ground construct complex nests that resemble

WEIRD WORLD

AN ANT SUPERCOLONY WAS FOUND IN JAPAN. IT CONTAINED MORE THAN 300 MILLION WORKERS LIVING IN 45,000 LINKED NESTS.

A PROCESSION OF LEAF-CUTTER ANTS CARRIES BITS OF VEGETATION BACK TO THE NEST TO FERTILIZE THEIR FUNGUS GARDEN.

40

miniature cities. After a queen ant has mated, she hunts for a crack in the soil and digs a little chamber. Here she lays her first batch of eggs and guards them until they hatch.

When the first worker ants emerge, the new colony gets seriously busy. The worker ants turn the area into a construction zone as they dig down to create a maze of tunnels and chambers.

The main chamber belongs to the egg-laying queen. Around this are chambers for the rest of the colony. Some just have eggs in them, others contain larvae, and a third type holds only pupae. Workers move the young between the different chambers as they grow.

Subterranean gardens

Leaf-cutter ants are great gardeners! It may sound odd, but these ants actually grow their own food – fungus. The ants tend fungus gardens in their underground nests. They grow the fungus on a fertilizer made from chewed-up leaves mixed with ant dung. When a queen leaves to found a new nest, she carries a tiny piece of fungus with her to start a new fungus garden.

Ant heap

Some ant colonies create mounds on top of their nests. Most spectacular are the piles of

LOG ON...
kidscience.about.com/
kids/kidscience/cs/insects/

pine needles that wood ants stack up. For a big colony of 100,000 ants the pile, which looks like a thatched roof, may be waist high. Wood ants prey on other insects, and a single colony may hunt down thousands of victims each day.

Two rulers

Only termite colonies have both a queen and king. The queen lays the eggs, and the king fertilizes them. (In social wasps, ants, and bees, the male who fertilizes the queen's eggs dies before the colony is founded.) Day and night, for most of her long life, the queen lays an egg every few seconds. In becoming a full-time egg factory, she swells up like a fat, white sausage. Too big to move, she relies entirely on the workers to feed and care for her.

Termite mounds

The tallest of all insect structures are termite mounds. The nests of African termites often reach a height of 25 ft (7.5 m). The human equivalent

THIS STRANGE MOUND WAS BUILT BY A SPECIES OF AFRICAN TERMITE. THE WEIRD, UMBRELLA-SHAPED CAPS MAY PROTECT THE NEST AGAINST TORRENTIAL RAINSTORMS.

TENDED BY WORKERS, A BLOATED TERMITE QUEEN MAY LAY 30,000 EGGS PER DAY. THE BIG TERMITE IN FRONT OF HER IS THE KING.

of this would be building a skyscraper 6 miles (9.6 km) high! Each towering mound is made from pellets of soil mixed with termite saliva. It's quite a feat, especially as worker termites are blind!

A termite tower works like an air-conditioning unit. It sucks hot air from the nest below and allows cooler air from above to replace it. This prevents the termites from roasting in the heat created by millions of bustling bodies.

Under the tower sits the nest itself, which is up to 10 ft (3 m) across. It contains a den for the queen, nurseries for the larvae, and fungus gardens. Leading from the nest and up through the tower are branching tunnels. The workers widen or narrow the tunnels to adjust the speed of air flowing through the nest. This ensures that the temperature in the nest never varies by more than one degree.

SOLDIER TERMITES PROTECT THE TERMITE NEST FROM ATTACKERS.

PROUD PARENTS

By human standards, insects are poor parents – most abandon their eggs as soon as they're laid, so the young must fend for themselves. The one thing they are good at is having vast numbers of children. But insects setting out to start a big family need a special ingredient – romance!

Attracting a mate

When women and men want to be attractive, they wear perfume or aftershave. A similar thing happens in the insect world. Butterflies and moths are the real wizards of scent. Some male butterflies find partners by flying past a female and scattering sweet-smelling dust onto her. (Sweet smelling to another butterfly, that is.) The scent is so magical that the star-struck female lands and sits still, inviting the male to mate with her.

With moths, it's the females who give off romantic smells. A female emperor moth's scent is so bewitching that even a male emperor flying along minding his own business a few miles away can't resist. As soon as his antennae pick up traces of her perfume in the air, he zigzags off at full speed to track down the wearer and declare his romantic intentions.

BUTTERFLIES AND MOTHS USE THEIR ANTENNAE TO DETECT SMELLS. SOME MALE MOTHS CAN SMELL A FEMALE ALMOST 7 MILES (11 KM) AWAY.

WHEN A MALE CICADA SINGS, THE RAPID CLICKS HE MAKES ON HIS SOUND ORGANS ARE AMPLIFIED BY AIR SACS IN HIS BODY. THE RESULT IS A LOUD WHINING NOISE.

Love songs

When crickets chirp or cicadas sing, what they are up to is the insect version of serenading under a balcony. And the louder they chirp, the dreamier they sound to any would-be mate within hearing. A male cicada can belt out a song with the power of 100 decibels – that's louder than a vacuum cleaner going full blast! He "sings" by clicking away at incredible speed using drumlike organs called tymbals on either side of his abdomen.

The light of love

Fireflies are really beetles. They get their name because the males look for mates by flying through the night sky flashing lights from their abdomens. Eager females flash back to signal their acceptance. The lights are made by chemicals inside the fireflies' bodies.

Mating marathon

Once their courtship is over insects can mate. Most mating insects like to get things over quickly. But dragonflies and damselflies remain locked in a passionate embrace for up to 10 hours! They also perform some weird acrobatics. When an amorous male finds a willing female, he loops his abdomen around to

MATING DAMSELFLIES JOIN TO FORM A HEART SHAPE, WITH THE MALE (RIGHT) GRIPPING THE FEMALE'S NECK AND HER TAIL BENDING FORWARD.

45

A STINKBUG GUARDS HER EGGS, WHICH SHE HAS GLUED TO A PLANT STEM.

pouch on his abdomen using the tip of her tail.

Dangerous lunch date

When a male praying mantis goes courting, predators are the least of his worries. If he's not careful, he may end up being eaten for lunch by his lover! The female is larger than the male, and wellknown for biting off her suitor's head and devouring his body.

To try to escape this bizarre fate, the male moves toward her very cautiously. He waves his antennae, stamps his feet, and waggles his body to show his intentions are honorable. When he's close (but not too close), he leaps onto her back and out of reach of her spine-studded front legs. If he's successful, he can then mate without being eaten alive.

Throw-away eggs

Once insects have mated, their next job is to find places to lay their eggs. Many appear to have a careless attitude about it.

get a grip on her neck. The couple flies off together with the female in a firm neck lock. After a while they land. Then she curls her long body between her legs to collect sperm from a

46

A BLUEBOTTLE GETS ITS NAME FROM ITS METALLIC BLUE ABDOMEN. THIS ONE IS LAYING HER EGGS ON SOME ROTTING MEAT.

With a few twitches of her abdomen, a female stick insect sprinkles her eggs around like confetti. It looks as if she doesn't give a hoot about the tiny eggs. But by scattering them widely, she makes it very difficult for predators to find them.

Eggs in hiding

All insects try to place their eggs where there's plenty of food and shelter nearby. That's why a bluebottle fly likes to lay eggs on a decaying corpse. A dead mouse or bird provides a mountain of meat for the fly's maggots when they hatch.

An acorn-eating weevil takes a lot of time to give its eggs a good start in life. It drills a hole into a fresh acorn with its snout, then turns around and injects an egg into the bottom of the hole. The

THE HOUSEHOLD COCKROACH KEEPS ITS EGGS IN A SPECIAL CASE. THE EGG CASE HANGS FROM HER REAR, AND SHE LUGS IT AROUND UNTIL THE EGGS HATCH.

47

ALTHOUGH DESERTED BY THEIR PARENTS,
THESE BEETLE LARVAE ARE COVERED IN
HARD SPINES TO PROTECT THEM.

young weevil grub hatches
out and – oh joy – finds itself
living inside its own dinner!
Other insects take great
care to hide their eggs so they
won't be stolen. Some species
of water bug are just as good
at this as Easter Bunnies.
They stash their eggs away so
carefully in the stems of water
plants that they are invisible
to any would-be egg stealers.

Egg heroes

A few insects never leave
their eggs at all. They do their
best to defend them from any
creatures with an eggs-for-lunch
gleam in the eye. One example
is a tiny thrips that feeds
on fungus and lives in the rain
forests of Panama. (Thrips are
slender insects with two pairs
of narrow, hair-fringed wings.)
The female thrips not only
protects her eggs, but also stays
with them after they have
hatched. During the day she

WEIRD WORLD
MALE DANCE FLIES GIVE FOOD
PARCELS TO THEIR FEMALE MATES
AS "WEDDING PRESENTS." THE
GIFTS ARE INSECTS WRAPPED UP
IN SILK. SOME MALES CHEAT
THEIR LOVERS AND OFFER AN
EMPTY SILK PARCEL!

APHIDS BEAR LIVE YOUNG AND REPRODUCE WITHOUT MATING

Super mom

A mother earwig digs a small hole in the soil under stones and lays 20 to 50 pearl-white eggs in it. While she waits for them to hatch, she turns them regularly and cleans off dirt and harmful fungus. If a predator comes too close, she threatens the intruder by fiercely waving her sharp pincers at it.

After the eggs hatch she stays at the nest and feeds her young by vomiting up food from her stomach. Baby earwigs usually stay with their mother for a week or so until they can fend for themselves. But if home proves too cozy and they don't want to leave, mom has a good way of persuading them to move out — she tries to eat them!

exceptions. The male giant water bug allows the female to glue batches of eggs onto his back. The eggs stay attached to dad until they hatch. He carries them around and strokes them to keep them clean. It's a tough job, because the eggs slow him

TO REPEL ATTACKERS WHO TRY TO REACH HER YOUNG, A FEMALE STINKBUG GIVES OFF A POWERFUL, VILE-SMELLING SCENT.

A BUTTERFLY STEPS OUT OF THE
PUPA IN WHICH IT CHANGED
FROM A LONG, LOOPING
CATERPILLAR INTO A
STYLISH-LOOKING
ADULT.

down so much that he
can't even feed while he
is hauling them around.

Fight for survival

Insect parents need to produce
lots of young to ensure that
some survive to become adults
and carry on the family line.
(Young insects make nutritious
snacks for birds, frogs, and a
whole range of other animals.)
Young froghopper bugs have
found that one of the
best ways to avoid
being gobbled
up is to
stay out of sight.
The froghoppers
blow a frothy liquid out of their
rear as they feed on plant sap.
Soon they are entirely covered
in foam and hidden from view.
We call this foam "cuckoo spit."

Growing up

As a young insect grows from
egg to adult, it sheds its skin
several times to produce a

larger exoskeleton. Insects such as cockroaches, crickets, true bugs, earwigs, and damselflies, are all born looking pretty much like their parents. We say they go through "incomplete metamorphosis" in order to become adults. This is a long-winded way of explaining that they don't change very much as they shed their skins and get bigger. Mostly they just sprout a set of wings and get larger appetites. About one in 10 of all insects develops in this way.

Big change

Nine out of 10 newborn insects become adults by going through "complete metamorphosis." This means that they change dramatically as they grow up. The larva that hatches from the egg looks no more like its mom and dad than a worm resembles a hedgehog. When it gets to the right size, the larva sheds its skin for the last time. The new skin hardens into a protective shell called a chrysalis. (Some insects spin a silken bag, or cocoon, around the chrysalis.) In this state, called a pupa, it rests quietly while its old body breaks down and a new, adult body is built.

AS A DAMSELFLY SHEDS ITS SKIN FOR THE LAST TIME, IT PUMPS BLOOD INTO ITS NEWLY FORMED WINGS TO EXPAND THEM TO THEIR FULL SIZE.

It emerges from the pupa looking completely different.

Insects that undergo this larva–pupa–adult change of life include beetles, flies, ants, bees, wasps, moths, and butterflies.

A YOUNG FROGHOPPER'S FROTHY COAT KEEPS ITS SOFT BODY FROM DRYING OUT.

GOOD SENSE

Insects don't have much in the brain department. An insect brain contains anything from a few thousand brain cells to just over a million, depending on the species. Humans, by contrast, have hundreds of billions of brain cells. However, insects make up for their tiny thoughts by having unbelievably good senses.

Enormous eyes

As much as 80 percent of an insect's brain is devoted to processing information from its eyes and antennae. That may sound like a lot, but it's understandable when you consider the size of some insect's eyes. A dragonfly's eyes, for example, take up most of the space on its head, just like hair does on your own. In fact, dragonfly eyes are so big

WITH HUGE EYES THAT WRAP RIGHT AROUND ITS HEAD, A DRAGONFLY HAS NEARLY ALL-AROUND VISION.

A COMMON WASP HAS THREE SIMPLE EYES ON TOP OF ITS HEAD AND A BIG, BULGING COMPOUND EYE ON EACH SIDE.

SIMPLE EYE

COMPOUND EYE

and bulgy that they almost meet at the top of the head.

This enables a dragonfly perched on a reed to peer up, down, ahead, and behind without ever having to move its head. It's a great trick, and it helps dragonflies to be ruthless hunters of other insects.

In fact, dragonflies' eyesight is so good that they can still catch mosquitoes at dusk, when our own eyes wouldn't be able to see a thing in the gloom.

Extra eyes

Humans have two eyes, both pretty much the same. Insects can have four, five, or even more eyes dotted around their heads, and they are not at all alike.

The smallest of them are known as simple eyes, which consist of a layer of light-sensitive cells. Simple eyes can tell the difference between light and shade, but they can't form images. That job is left to the larger eyes, which are called compound eyes. Each compound eye is packed with hundreds, or even thousands, of tiny lenses – nearly 30,000 in the case of some dragonflies. We do not know exactly what insects see with their compound eyes, but

WEIRD WORLD

SOME NOCTURNAL INSECTS CAN DETECT A LIGHT SOURCE EVEN WHEN THEIR EYES HAVE BEEN COVERED UP. THIS IS BECAUSE THEY ALSO HAVE TINY LIGHT SENSORS DOTTED OVER THE SURFACE OF THEIR BODIES.

we do know that they are incredibly good at detecting movement – which is one reason why insects tend to be so difficult to catch!

Although insect larvae usually only have simple eyes, most adults have compound eyes as

ITS LEG BASKETS BULGING WITH POLLEN, A HONEYBEE USES ITS ULTRAVIOLET VISION TO HOME IN ON ANOTHER FLOWER.

well. A wasp, for example, has three simple eyes arranged in a triangle on top of its head, and a compound eye on either side. The simple eyes may help the wasp to balance as it flies around.

Supervision

Insect eyes can see things that are invisible to humans. One of the things they can see is ultraviolet light – the part of the Sun's light that can give people sunburn. Many flowers have patterns of lines that show up in

WEIRD WORLD

A WORKER HONEYBEE PERFORMS A SPECIAL DANCE TO TELL OTHER BEES WHERE TO FIND FOOD. THE WATCHING BEES ALSO SAMPLE FLOWER SCENTS ON ITS BODY AND NECTAR THAT IT VOMITS UP.

THESE TWO WORKER ANTS ARE COMMUNICATING BY TOUCHING FEELERS. THEY EXCHANGE SCENTS THAT ACT LIKE CHEMICAL MESSAGES.

LOG ON... www.insecta.com has a "bug of the month"

talking about noses. Insects smell with their antennae, which are covered in tiny, scent-detecting hairs. Because antennae are also used for touch (which is why we often call them "feelers"), it's probably a little like smelling the world with your fingertips.

ultraviolet light. The lines, which are called honey guides, lead insects to the flowers' nectar. Insects can see honey guides in broad daylight. The honey guides help the insects to make a "beeline" for the food. Humans can see honey guides only if all the other colors in daylight are kept out – something that only happens in the laboratory.

F eels smelly

Don't be fooled into thinking that all insects have good eyesight. Ants' eyes are very weak – in fact, many ants are blind. Yet they get around with no problem at all because they have a terrific sense of smell. But when we're talking of smell in the insect world, we're not

A nt communication

When two ants meet, the first thing they do is to stroke one another's antennae to feel and smell what the other ant has to say. As the feelers brush, they swap scents that are messages about food, eggs, danger, and other gossip to do with

LONGHORN BEETLES HAVE SMALL EYES BUT LONG ANTENNAE UP TO FOUR TIMES THE LENGTH OF THEIR BODIES.

55

the ant colony. One scent could be a message that means "Let's carry that dead ant out of the nest." Another scent might be a rallying cry that says "Call up the troops to defend the nest!" Yet another could be a warning signal to tell everyone to flee from danger.

A similar thing happens in a beehive. When a honeybee is attacked or injured, it gives off a special scent. Other bees smell it and react as if an alarm bell has rung. They buzz around angrily and get ready to sting anything nearby that looks like it is going to attack the hive.

T aste detectors

If smelling with your fingertips sounds odd, how about tasting with your feet? This is what insects can do, because they have special taste-detecting hairs on their feet as well as on their mouthparts.

What use is that? Well, let's look at the cabbage white butterfly. A female cabbage white prefers to lay her eggs on cabbages, because they are the favorite food of her fussy larvae. She can tell cabbages apart from other plants by the taste of the mustard oil that their leaves give off. When she lands on a leaf, she just has to stamp up and down to find out if it's the right kind of plant to lay eggs on.

WITH BIG COMPOUND EYES AND BRISTLING WITH SENSE HAIRS, FLIES ARE WELL-EQUIPPED TO MAKE OUT THE WORLD AROUND THEM.

WHEN SOME MOTHS HEAR A BAT, THEY FOLD UP THEIR WINGS AND PLUMMET TO THE GROUND TO AVOID BEING EATEN.

Touch and movement

As well as sense hairs for smelling and tasting, insects also have tiny hairs on their bodies that are sensitive to touch and which can detect vibrations in the air. When these hairs are bent – by an object or moving air – they send nerve signals to the insect's brain.

By detecting vibrations in the air caused by the movement of other animals, an insect can tell if an attacker is approaching or its prey running away.

caused by landing too hard after a long jump, it's actually an ear, and it's used to listen for the mating songs of other crickets.

Having ears in weird places is common among insects. In praying mantises, the ears are on the thorax, while lacewings and some moths have theirs on the wings. The ears of cicadas,

SOME FLIES CAN SMELL ROTTING FLESH FROM SEVERAL MILES AWAY

Listen up

Like us, insects are able to hear sounds, but they don't have an ear sticking out from each side of the head. Crickets have a big swelling below the knees of each front leg. Although the swelling looks like a bump

grasshoppers, and other moths are on the abdomens.

Some moths can use their ears to eavesdrop on the high-pitched sounds that hunting bats make. If they are lucky, it gives the moths time to dodge out of the way and escape.

SHAPE AND COLOR

Like spies in disguise, insects go to great lengths not to be caught. The best way to avoid ending up in the belly of a predator is to stay out of sight. By adapting their shape and color, insects have developed some cunning tricks to escape the gaze of sharp-eyed hunters.

Concealed by camouflage
Using color and shape to blend in with the surroundings is called camouflage. It can be very simple, such as the way a green grasshopper is hidden among plants by its green color. But some insects have turned camouflage into an art form. Their fantastic color patterns and weird shapes enable them to become pretty much invisible against particular backgrounds.

THE GIANT LEAF INSECT LOOKS LIKE A SLIGHTLY SHRIVELED LEAF, COMPLETE WITH HOLES.

A MERVEILLE DU JOUR MOTH IS EASY TO SPOT ON TREE BARK, BUT IT DISAPPEARS AGAINST A BACKGROUND OF LICHEN.

Lichen lovers
Lots of insects have discovered that tree trunks make great places to hide. Some Central American flatid bugs have see-through bodies. When they rest on tree bark, a predator sees the bark underneath, not the bug itself. Many beetles and moths lie low on lichen – a papery, funguslike stuff that grows on tree trunks. Their mottled markings perfectly match the lichen's brown and white colors, so they melt away from view.

Leaves and sticks
Leaf insects have flattened abdomens and leg segments that give them a remarkable

Weird World

One type of moth disguises itself as bird poop! When it sits on a leaf, the spreading white hairs on its legs give it the shape of a splattered bird dropping.

look just like a normal twig. Most camouflage works on the principle that if you stay still, you won't be spotted. But on a breezy day, with trees and bushes swaying, standing dead still might give you away. So, the stick insect rocks its body gently to and fro, like a twig blowing in the wind.

Thorn bugs

Another type of camouflage is to dress up as something inedible. That's what some treehopper bugs do. They have a pointed extension to the thorax that makes them the spitting image of thorns. These "thorn bugs," as they are also known, cluster on plants, where they feed on plant sap, happy in the knowledge that they are of no interest to hungry birds. After all, who'd want to eat thorns? The only time that the bugs move is to find a new feeding spot.

resemblance to leaves. Their markings imitate the ribs and veins of leaves, while the edges of the body may be brown and crisp, like a dying leaf. The excellent disguise conceals them from predators, but there's always a small risk that they might end up getting munched by a plant-eater by mistake! As it sits contentedly in a tree or bush, a stick insect's long, slender body and legs make it

Warning colors

Some insects don't care two hoots if hunters know where they are. They go out of their way to be seen by having bold markings and snazzy colors. They seem to be saying, "Hey, over here! It's me!" That's because they are either loaded with poison or pack such a powerful sting or

passionflower vines. It sounds romantic, but it doesn't make the caterpillars sweet to eat. The leaves are rich in cyanide, and this deadly poison ends up stored in the caterpillars' spiky

ONE GRASSHOPPER LOOKS JUST LIKE A LUMP OF QUARTZITE ROCK

bite that few animals ever dare to tangle with them. Orange, black, yellow, and red are often used to warn other animals to steer clear of an insect.

P oisonous postman
Postman caterpillars feed on the leaves of

THE POSTMAN CATERPILLAR'S POISONOUS SPIKES HELP TO DETER BIRDS FROM ATTACKING.

bodies. The brightly decorated postman caterpillars go around with an "eat me and drop dead" attitude. It's good advertising, and it gets noticed – birds never touch them more than once!

Insect mimics

Lots of harmless insects have taken to copying the looks of insects that sting or contain vile-tasting chemicals. It's a clever way of enjoying the bad reputation of another insect without the hard work! These copycats are called mimics. Hoverflies, for example, are wasp and bumblebee mimics. They look and hover like wasps and bumblebees, so few animals attack them for fear of getting stung.

Not all mimics copy insects. One weevil in New Guinea has discovered that life is a lot safer if it acts like a spider. Although

HOVERFLY   WASP

THIS HOVERFLY (LEFT) IS ABOUT THE SAME COLOR, SIZE, AND SHAPE AS A COMMON WASP (RIGHT). HOWEVER, THE HOVERFLY HAS TWO WINGS AND THE WASP FOUR.

THE WINGS OF THIS BANANA-EATING BUTTERFLY FROM NEW GUINEA CARRY LARGE EYESPOTS FOR STARTLING PREDATORS.

it has six legs to a spider's eight, it still runs around like a spider and holds its legs in a spidery way. This simple trick improves its chances of surviving.

Shock tactics

Sometimes it's better to hotfoot it out of tricky situations, rather than to sit still and hope that you're not seen. To aid their escape, some insects have a large eye-shaped spot on each wing. If disturbed, they spread their wings and flash these eyespots. The startled attacker thinks it has picked on a larger animal than it bargained for. The insect wins a split-second chance to make its getaway.

Act menacing

Predators can often be deterred if their potential prey puts on a menacing display.

THE PUSS MOTH CATERPILLAR LASHES ITS WHIPLIKE "TAILS" TO AND FRO TO MAKE ATTACKERS THINK THEY ARE STINGS.

The puss moth caterpillar has a red ring and black eyespots at the front of its thorax. When threatened, it pulls its head back into its thorax, creating a hideous, facelike pattern. If a bird sees it rearing up and swaying menacingly like an angry snake, it backs off and the caterpillar survives to see another day.

63

FEEDING FRENZY

Why is a group of hungry kids like a swarm of locusts? The answer is that both can empty a fridge in less than a minute! The kids, we hope, would be polite enough to use knives and forks when they eat. Since bugs don't care for cutlery, they have a range of mouthparts to get food into their bellies.

Two pairs of jaws

The shape of an insect's mouthparts depends entirely on its eating habits. Insects that chew their food – including beetles, grasshoppers, and termites – have a pair of jaws called mandibles. The jaws have serrated edges, rather like the teeth of a saw. These powerful tools move sideways to cut and grind up hunks of food. Behind the mandibles lie a second pair of jaws, called maxillae, which are not quite as powerful. The maxillae are mostly used to line up the food ready to push it on its way into the insect's abdomen. But why bother to give yourself a jaw

AFTER THESE HORSEFLIES HAVE GORGED THEMSELVES ON BLOOD, THEY WILL FLY OFF, LEAVING PAINFUL WOUNDS BEHIND.

ache chewing when you can suck, sip, or slurp your food…

B loodsuckers

Lots of insects like to take their meals the easy way – as a drink. Animal blood is a nourishing, protein-filled food drunk by horseflies and other bloodsucking insects. Once a female horsefly finds an animal, she chases after it. When she lands, she slashes open the skin with her curved, swordlike jaws. Next she uses a sharp rod to drill up and down to get the blood flowing. As she sucks the blood up through her mouth tube, she pumps saliva into the wound to prevent the blood from clotting.

What's the male horsefly doing while this bloodthirsty business is going on? Probably sitting on a flower somewhere drinking nectar, because it's only the females that have biting mouthparts and feed on blood.

N ectar sippers

Moths and butterflies carry a long tongue (known as a proboscis) rolled up like a length of fire hose under the head. After they land on a flower, muscles in the head start to pump blood into the tongue. It uncoils and reaches down into the base of the flower where the sugary nectar is stored. Then the butterfly takes a dainty sip.

BUTTERFLIES HAVE NO JAWS, JUST A TUBELIKE TONGUE THAT STAYS COILED UP WHEN NOT IN USE.

Sap slurpers

True bugs have mouths shaped like the needles doctors use for injections. Many, including cicadas, treehoppers, and aphids, use this little syringe to punch a hole in a plant so they can drink the mineral-rich sap inside. Aphids tap the veins of plants where the sap flows

strongest. In fact, the sap flows so powerfully that the aphids hardly have to slurp at all. They glug down so much that sap spouts out of their rear end as honeydew. This is the sweet syrup that ants adore.

Liquidize your enemies

Some insects that enjoy liquid lunches are ruthless killers. The robberfly snatches other insects in midair with ease. From its perch on a rock or a twig, the robberfly rockets upward, grabs a flying insect with its spiny feet, and lands for the feast. Its mouth stabs into the victim's body and injects saliva, which quickly dissolves the innards. After sucking out the mushy liquid, it takes off

A BRAZILIAN SHIELD BUG DRINKS SAP FROM A PLANT STEM. SOME SAP SLURPERS, SUCH AS APHIDS, CAN PASS HARMFUL VIRUSES BETWEEN PLANTS AS THEY FEED.

nest construction and to handle building materials, while their tubelike proboscis is normally used to feed on nectar. But some hunting wasps use their jaws to squeeze the body fluids from their victims, which they then suck up.

leaving behind the lifeless, shriveled body of its prey.

Dual-purpose mouths
Wasps and bees have both biting and sucking mouthparts. The biting jaws are used for

A ROBBERFLY STABS
ITS VICTIM BETWEEN
THE HEAD
AND THORAX.
DEATH IS
ALMOST
INSTANT.

CLUTCHING A TWIG WITH ITS PROLEGS, AN OAK SILKMOTH CATERPILLAR MAKES SHORT WORK OF ANOTHER LEAF. ITS JAWS WORK FROM SIDE TO SIDE AS IT CHEWS THROUGH THE LEAVES AND STEMS OF OAK TREES.

WEIRD WORLD
THE LONGEST INSECT TONGUE IN THE WORLD BELONGS TO DARWIN'S HAWKMOTH OF MADAGASCAR. MEASURING 11 IN (28 CM) TO THE TIP, IT IS USED TO SIP NECTAR FROM THE DEEP FLOWER TUBES OF STAR ORCHIDS.

Spit soup
Houseflies probably have the most disgusting eating habits of all insects. When a fly lands on something good (it can tell the flavor using taste buds on its feet), it says "yum" to itself and promptly vomits all over it! The fly's saliva digests the food and turns it into a soupy liquid. The fly mops it all up with the spongy pad at the end of its mouth tube. So, next time a cute little fly appears to kiss a piece of food, remember what it's really doing!

Leaf crunchers
A liquid diet isn't to the taste of all insects. Many prefer solid food such as crunchy leaves. The chief leaf-eaters are grasshoppers, leaf beetles, katydids, and the caterpillars of butterflies and moths. Caterpillars are often called "feeding machines," because they have to eat continually while they

are larvae, so they can store up enough proteins in their bodies for egg laying as adults. Their mouthparts are perfect for making mincemeat out of leaves. The jaws have overlapping edges that slice up leaves like scissors and grinding plates to mash every mouthful to a pulp.

Digestive aids

You may not think that wood is very appetizing, but it's perfect for meeting the daily needs of insects such as wood termites and wood-boring beetles. Most animals can't digest cellulose, which is one of the main ingredients of wood. But these insects can survive on a diet of wood because they have microbes (tiny, single-celled organisms called protozoa and bacteria) living in their digestive systems. In return for a cozy home

in an insect's belly, the microbes make chemicals called enzymes, which break down the cellulose into much simpler substances that the insect can digest.

Meat-eaters

Some insects, including ground beetles, mantises, and many ants, enjoy nothing better than to tuck into a chunk of fresh meat. The fiercest and fastest of all ground beetles is the tiger beetle. Like every other meat-eating beetle, it has two sets of jaws – a set of big jaws for chopping up victims and a set of smaller ones for stuffing

THE TIGER BEETLE HAS SHARP
EYESIGHT. IT CHASES PREY
BY SPRINTING ON ITS
LONG LEGS AND MAKING
SHORT FLIGHTS WITH
ITS WINGS.

69

THESE TREEHOPPERS DON'T MIND BEING TENDED BY ANTS, AS IT ALSO CLEANS THEM. IF THEY WERE LEFT ALONE, THEIR HONEYDEW WOULD GO MOLDY AND SLOWLY SUFFOCATE THEM.

all the bits and pieces into its mouth. The tiger beetle lurks in a burrow until an unsuspecting creature, say a grasshopper or slug, comes near. Then it charges and pounces. The last thing the struggling victim sees is a huge pair of jaws being wielded like a set of garden shears!

K iller ants

Most ants are meat-eaters. Each day, ants catch billions of other insects. Prey is killed by being stung, bitten, or just stretched and pulled to death. Small victims may be dragged back to the nest by individual ants. But larger prey may require a team of workers to chop it up into more manageable pieces.

S weet tooth

Ants adore sweet things just as much as savory snacks. Groups of ants can often be seen tending bugs such as aphids or treehoppers, because they love the sugary honeydew that the bugs produce. The ants stroke the bugs with their antennae to make them give off more. Then they slurp up the drops of liquid that leak out of the bugs' rear ends. Ants have such a sweet tooth that they will happily defend a group of bugs against other insects. They may even go so far as to build little shelters for the bugs in order to keep off the rain!

Living larders

Honeypot ants dwell in dry parts of North America. When food is plentiful, the ants feed some workers with vast amounts of nectar and honeydew, making

Zero calories

It sounds incredible, but there are some insects that eat nothing at all after becoming adults – they survive on zero calories! An adult mayfly doesn't eat a

ABOUT FIVE PERCENT OF ALL LEAVES ON EARTH GET EATEN BY INSECTS

them swell to the size of beads. Their abdomens get so bloated that they never leave the nest but stay underground, hanging from the walls and ceilings like tiny pots of honey. If drought sets in and food becomes scarce, the "honeypots" vomit up drops of honeydew to feed the other ants.

single meal (as a youngster it lives underwater and feeds on plants). Its adult life only lasts for a day or so, and during this time it is far too busy trying to find a mate to bother with food. The mayfly's gut is full of air, making it very light – which is handy, since it spends most of its short life on the wing.

ADULT MAYFLIES REACH OLD AGE BY THEIR FIRST EVENING. TO MAKE THE MOST OF SUCH A SHORT TIME ON EARTH, THEY NEVER STOP TO EAT.

71

INSECT WARS

No matter how tough an insect you are, there's always something out there that can get you. Being the favorite food of so many other types of animal is bad enough. But to make things worse, insects also wage war on each other, either to satisfy their hunger or to settle disputes over territory, food, or mates. Whatever the reason, the battles can be very brutal…and often deadly.

Wasps on the prowl

Hunting wasps are relatives of the hornets and common wasps that buzz around our picnics. Their stingers pack the same wallop, but they only use their weapons to slaughter other insects. When a female wasp catches her prey, the first thing she does is to inject her poison into it. This paralyzes but doesn't kill the victim. Then she carries the stiff but still-alive prey into a burrow. She lays an egg on top of the body and flies away. The whole operation is her way of doing a little advance food shopping for her baby. Later, when her larva hatches out, it will have plenty of fresh meat to eat, thanks to mom.

Hunting wasps are choosy. Some only attack spiders, while others hunt flies

A WEEVIL-HUNTING WASP PREYS ONLY ON WEEVILS. IT PARALYZES ITS VICTIMS BY STINGING THEM ON THE UNDERSIDE OF THE ABDOMEN.

WHITE SILK COCOONS SPUN BY PARASITIC
WASP LARVAE HANG FROM THE BACK OF
THIS CATERPILLAR'S BODY.

host's body.
As well as
eating their
poor host from
the inside out, they
also use its body as
a convenient place to
pupate. We don't know how
the host feels about all this,
but one thing's certain – the
hungry larvae eventually kill it.

LOG ON...
Watch ants live at
www.antcam.com/

or caterpillars. All the food that
they find is saved for the kids –
adults are strictly vegetarian.

P arasite perils

The best way to attack
your enemy is from the
inside. The larvae
of many
wasps are
parasites, which means
that they live and grow on
or inside another insect's
body. When it is
time to lay her eggs,
a female parasitic
wasp deposits them
on, or in, the living
bodies of another
insect. After the
eggs hatch, the
wasp larvae
munch away at
the delicious
innards of their

E ggs within eggs

Like hunting wasps, different
parasitic wasps attack different
kinds of insects. Lots go for big,
soft targets like the caterpillars
of moths and butterflies. Others
hunt the larvae of beetles and
flies. Many tiny wasps, called
chalcids, can't resist attacking
the eggs of other insects. They
lay their eggs inside eggs that
were laid earlier. Their
young always

A FEMALE
ICHNEUMON WASP
DRILLS INTO WOOD
WITH HER LONG
EGG-LAYING TUBE.
THEN SHE LAYS AN EGG
ON A BEETLE GRUB
INSIDE THE WOOD.

hatch first, so they have plenty of time to eat up the egg in which they find themselves.

All-out war

Sometimes insect battles are on a grand scale, with hundreds or thousands of individuals involved. Like everything else ants do, when they go to war they set out in large numbers – and termite nests are favorite targets of many ant species. The ant raiders pour into every hole and crack in a termite nest, seizing workers and young and carrying them off to be eaten.

Although termites don't have stings, they do have their own ways of fighting back. Soldier termites are much bigger than workers and have enlarged heads. Some can dismember an ant with a single flick of their huge jaws. Others have short, flat heads that they use to plug holes in the nest and stop the raiders from getting in. Snouted termites can spray irritating chemicals from their extended snouts. There are even soldier

ANTS AND TERMITES HAVE BEEN DEADLY ENEMIES FOR MILLIONS OF YEARS. HERE, AN ANT ATTACKS A SOLDIER TERMITE.

AN ASSASSIN BUG IMPALES A GRASSHOPPER ON ITS DAGGERLIKE BEAK AFTER A SUCCESSFUL AMBUSH.

termites that turn themselves into suicide bombers. They squeeze their abdominal muscles to fire a volley of sticky goo out of their mouths at attackers. Occasionally, the muscles may squeeze so hard that the termite's body explodes!

Ambush specialists

All this rushing around fighting is far too much effort for some insects. Many assassin bugs are ambush specialists who prefer to sit patiently on leaves, bark, or flowers, waiting for an insect to come within pouncing range. With lightning-fast reflexes, a hiding assassin bug grabs its surprised victim and plunges its long beak deep into the body to kill the prey.

Trap-setting killers

Some sit-and-wait killers set clever traps to ensure that they get their victims. To attract flies that feed on animal droppings, one type of rove beetle both looks and smells like dung. A hungry fly arriving for dinner soon finds itself being eaten as the main course!

An ant lion is the larva of an insect like a damselfly. To catch prey, it digs a funnel-shaped pit in sandy soil. Lurking at the bottom, it hurls sand grains at passing ants and other insects, causing them to fall into the pit and straight into its spiky jaws.

75

Family feuds

Being attacked by complete strangers is normal in the insect world. But some insects also get into serious fights with members of their own species.

A male stag beetle patrols and defends his home patch, which is usually a log or a tree branch. This is where he courts a female and where she lays her eggs. If a rival male wanders up, hoping to steal the beetle's mate, a fight breaks out. The two males waltz about trying to grab each other around the middle with their huge jaws. The first to get a good grip lifts his opponent off the ground and flips him onto his back.

If he can, he shoves the beetle off the branch and lets him drop to the ground. The loser rarely gets killed (he has hard wing cases to protect his body) but the victor always gets the girl!

Aerial combat

A male dragonfly ferociously guards his property, which may be a stretch of riverbank or a clump of reeds. When another

STAG BEETLE FIGHTS ARE TRIALS OF STRENGTH. BUT IF THE DEFEATED BEETLE ENDS UP ON HIS BACK, HE MAY BE DEVOURED BY ANTS BEFORE HE CAN RIGHT HIMSELF.

THIS TIGER MOTH CATERPILLAR
HAS A SOFT, FURRY APPEARANCE
– BUT IT'S JUST A TRICK. IF YOU
TOUCH IT, THE YELLOW
HAIRS BREAK OFF AND
STICK INTO YOUR SKIN.

male invades
his territory, he
circles the intruder,
flashing his bright colors.
If this doesn't deter his rival, a
clash occurs. Sometimes, one of
the males gets knocked into the
water and drowns.

Noise annoys

Cracker butterflies are far more
stylish. If a male cracker gets
annoyed with another male in
his patch, he snaps his wings
violently to make a cracking
sound. He dances around the
intruder, snapping furiously
to drive it away. The dispute
is settled without any
fighting or injury –
just damaged pride!

Fighting back

Insects use lots of tricks to
get back at the bullies and
enemies that plague their lives.

The simplest form of
defense is to adopt a
threatening posture.
The weta, a large

New Zealand cricket, does just
that. If the attacker doesn't take
the hint and back off, it risks a
nasty wound from the weta's
spine-studded hind legs.

The next best thing
is to make yourself
untouchable. Some
caterpillars are clad
in brittle hairs that

A WETA RAISES ITS HIND LEGS
IN A THREATENING POSE.

THE BOMBARDIER BEETLE CAN SWIVEL THE END OF ITS ABDOMEN TO POINT ITS SPRAY IN ANY DIRECTION. IT CAN SWITCH THE SPRAY ON AND OFF 500 TIMES A SECOND.

The spray is made up of two harmless chemicals that the beetle stores separately in its body. When it feels frightened, it squeezes the two chemicals into a special chamber. As the chemicals combine, there is a tiny explosion that shoots a jet of hot liquid and gas from

break off easily and lodge in an enemy's skin or mouth. If swallowed, the caterpillar soon finds itself spat out again – few predators enjoy painful dinners!

Chemical defenses
The most cunning tricks use chemistry. A number of insects can fire toxic chemicals at their enemies. The best chemical gun of all belongs to the bombardier beetle, which blasts attackers such as birds, toads, spiders, and ants with a boiling spray.

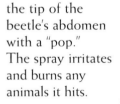

the tip of the beetle's abdomen with a "pop." The spray irritates and burns any animals it hits.

Blistering blood
Some beetles, grasshoppers, and other insects can ooze toxic fluids from their leg joints, mouth, or rear end when grabbed by a predator. This defence tactic is called "reflex bleeding." The fluids can blister an enemy's skin and cause severe internal burns if the predator dares to eat the beetle.

WEIRD WORLD
TOXIC OIL BEETLES USE "REFLEX BLEEDING" TO DEFEND THEMSELVES. WHEN HANDLED, THEY OOZE CANTHARIDIN – A POISON SO POWERFUL THAT A DOSE OF JUST 0.001 OZ (0.003 G) IS FATAL TO HUMANS.

THIS FUNGUS BEETLE DEFENDS ITSELF BY "BLEEDING" HARMFUL CHEMICALS FROM ITS LEG JOINTS.

Hiss or squeak

Insects can't cry for help, but they can still make sounds to startle attackers. The Madagascan hissing cockroach, for meat-eaters steer clear of dead insects – they prefer prey to be alive and kicking. Click beetles are good at playing dead. If it's threatened, a click beetle pulls in its legs and topples off its tree to the ground. It lies there on its back, perfectly still, until the attacker goes away. If the enemy isn't fooled, the beetle hurls itself up to 12 in (30 cm) into

A BOMBARDIER'S SPRAY IS UP TO 212°F (100°C)

example, produces a loud hiss by forcing air out of the breathing holes, called spiracles, along its abdomen. There is also a beetle, called the screech beetle, that squeaks when it is picked up.

the air with a loud "click." The beetle makes its escape, while the bemused predator wonders what on Earth's going on!

Drop dead

If all else fails, playing dead is always worth a try. This can work because many

CLICK BEETLES CATAPULT THEMSELVES INTO THE AIR USING A SPRINGLIKE DEVICE ON THEIR BODIES.

INSECTS ON TRIAL

Are insects a good or a bad thing? If you've just been stung by a wasp or scared out of your wits by a big, hairy spider, you'll probably want to squash every insect on Earth! But before you pass judgment on these poor little critters, let's look at the evidence for and against creepy crawlies as we put insects on trial.

Accidental killer

People have lots of reasons for not liking insects – and getting bitten by them is high on the list. Most of us know how miserably painful or irritating it can be if we're bitten by midges, horseflies, black flies, bedbugs, fleas, and a host of other bloodthirsty creatures. Apart from a bite mark, some insects leave a nasty gift behind when they leave – disease.

Believe it or not, mosquitoes are the biggest killers of humans on the planet (apart from other humans, that is). Every year, mosquitoes inject malaria germs into 200 million people, while more than three million die of the disease. Mosquitoes don't do it deliberately. It's just that the

A MOSQUITO INJECTS AN ANAESTHETIC INTO YOUR BODY SO THAT YOU CAN'T FEEL IT SUCKING YOUR BLOOD.

germs accidentally get passed on from person to person when they feed on human blood. The germs are carried in saliva that the mosquito injects into the wound made by its needlelike mouthparts. It is said that every 10 seconds someone somewhere in the world dies of malaria from a mosquito bite.

Disease spreaders

Unfortunately for us, mosquitoes are just the tip of the iceberg. There are plenty of other insects that spread illness and disease among humans. Clothes lice spread typhus, tsetse flies infect people with sleeping sickness, black-rat fleas spread plague, to name just a few of the villains. Don't panic, because doctors have a whole arsenal of drugs with which they can fight these diseases. But there's a long way to go before the battle's won.

happily destroy the timbers of our homes, clothes moths eat our favorite garments, booklice munch away at our papers and books, and there's plenty of others who've got their eyes on the contents of our kitchen cabinets. And those pesky pests are also out there in gardens and farms gobbling up our crops…

Pests indoors

Not content with attacking our bodies, insects also wreak havoc in our homes and demolish our possessions. Termites, deathwatch beetles, and woodworm beetles very

TWO CLOTHES MOTHS SIT UNSEEN ON A SWEATER. THE OVAL COCOONS SPUN BY THE LARVAE ARE CAMOUFLAGED WITH WOOL

P ests outdoors

If you were a farmer and woke one morning to find that all the buds and leaves of your potato plants were gone, then what you'd probably say as you sobbed at the sight is, "*#$!@£!* Colorado beetles!" These fat little beetles are the world's worst potato pests. Originally from western North America, they are now found wherever potatoes are an important crop. Both adults and larvae feast on the leaves of the plants, and they are very hard to control with chemical sprays.

Insects damage crops all the time. But now and then they break out as plagues that catch farmers by surprise. In 1991, an outbreak of silverleaf whitefly in the South swept through fields of melons, tomatoes, cotton, and other crops. By the time the pest was brought under control, it had caused half a billion dollars' worth of damage to farmers.

T hey're not all bad

You'll be glad to hear that only 1 in 100 insect species does us any harm, and many of the rest are positively helpful to us. The most important job they do is to pollinate plants. It happens when they fly or crawl into a flower to feed. While doing it, they get dusted with pollen. When they climb into the next flower, the pollen rubs off so that new seeds and fruits can form. If insects didn't pollinate plants, we would soon starve. We'd run out of berries, plums, cauliflowers, cucumbers, and pears to start with. And you would certainly never again have apples in your lunchbox!

P est controllers

The best way to beat back the billions of bugs that go for crops is to use other insects to prey on them. It's a lot cheaper than chemical sprays and better for the environment too. Hunters, like ladybugs and

LADYBUGS PREY ON SOFT-BODIED INSECT PESTS. FARMERS AND GARDENERS USE THEM AS NATURAL PEST CONTROLLERS.

wasps, kill millions of aphids and caterpillars every day that would otherwise be eating what we grow.

Garbage collectors

Another really amazing thing that insects do is to dispose of most of the garbage from our planet. Imagine if dung and dead plants and animals were left to lie around – we'd very soon be buried under a foul mountain of rot and poop! Luckily, plenty of insects get their kicks from devouring this unpleasant stuff.

Really useful

Insects also supply us with many useful products. Anyone who has ever slurped honey, worn a silk shirt, used food coloring, or varnished wood has insects to thank.

WEIRD WORLD

EACH YEAR, ABOUT 20 PERCENT OF ALL THE GRAIN, FRUIT, AND VEGETABLE CROPS THAT WE GROW ENDS UP IN THE BELLIES OF INSECTS. NO WONDER FARMERS SPEND SO MUCH ON PESTICIDES!

Bees make honey. Silkmoth cocoons give us raw silk. Scale insects give us a red food dye called cochineal. And some wood varnishes contain shellac, a substance that comes from another type of scale insect that lives in Southeast Asia and India. Gooey stuff, called lac, oozes out of these insects. It is gathered, washed, processed, and used in wood varnish, or to bind together confectionaries and pills.

Really tasty

Be thankful for insects – they keep lots of other animals alive because they are a never-ending source of food. Bats catch flying insects. Anteaters break open ant nests to feast on their contents. Badgers and foxes dig up juicy grubs. Lizards and frogs snap at flies. Fish gulp down any insect that lands on water. Even baby alligators munch on them.

Delicious dishes

You may find it disgusting, but many people find insects tasty, too! After all, they're rich in energy, vitamins, and minerals. In Colombia people fry up big-bottomed ants for lunch, while in Taiwan silkmoth pupae are roasted and enjoyed as a treat. Aboriginal Australians have been barbecuing beetle and moth grubs for thousands of years. It's all good healthy stuff and not so different, really, from grilling insectlike shrimp and prawns fished from the sea.

So, you see, insect and human lives are so closely interwoven that – love 'em or hate 'em – we just can't live without them.

HERE'S A NOURISHING DISH OF CATERPILLARS. NOURISHING? YES, CATERPILLARS ARE ARE UP TO 70 PERCENT PROTEIN.

REFERENCE SECTION

Whether you've finished reading *Bugs*, or are turning to this section first, you'll find the information on the next eight pages really useful. Here are all the facts and figures, background details, and unfamiliar words that you will need. You'll also find a list of website addresses – so, whether you want to surf the net or search out facts, these pages should turn you from an enthusiast into an expert.

INSECT CLASSIFICATION

In order to discuss all the different species of plant and animal, scientists classify them into a series of categories according to the features that they share. The largest category is the kingdom. Insects are part of the animal kingdom, which also includes every other animal species. The kingdom is divided into smaller categories, which are further divided until individual species are reached. The smaller the category, the more features the animals in it have in common. The chart below shows the classification of the common red ant.

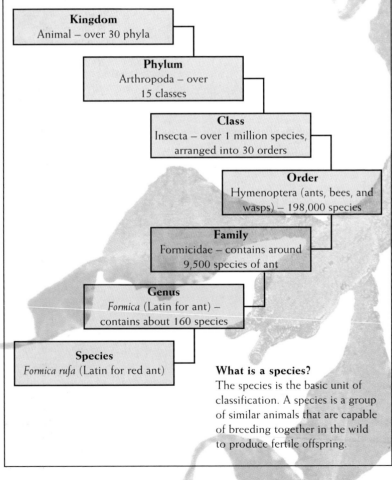

Kingdom
Animal – over 30 phyla

Phylum
Arthropoda – over
15 classes

Class
Insecta – over 1 million species,
arranged into 30 orders

Order
Hymenoptera (ants, bees, and
wasps) – 198,000 species

Family
Formicidae – contains around
9,500 species of ant

Genus
Formica (Latin for ant) –
contains about 160 species

Species
Formica rufa (Latin for red ant)

What is a species?
The species is the basic unit of classification. A species is a group of similar animals that are capable of breeding together in the wild to produce fertile offspring.

KEY INSECT ORDERS

This chart gives details of 24 of the most important orders of insects.

NAME	MEANING	EXAMPLES	SPECIES	FEATURES
Collembola	Sticky peg	Springtails	6,500	Simple, wingless insects with a forked springing organ for jumping.
Thysanura	Bristle tails	Silverfish	370	Long, wingless insects found in dark, damp places. Run fast when disturbed.
Ephemeroptera	Live for a day	Mayflies	2,500	Larvae live in fresh water. Adults don't eat, and only live for a day or two.
Odonata	Toothed flies	Dragonflies, damselflies	5,500	Large, strong fliers with huge eyes. Larvae are fresh-water predators.
Plecoptera	Wickerwork wings	Stone flies	2,000	Larvae live in fresh water, adults live along riverbanks. Adults eat plants or not at all.
Blattodea	Avoiding light	Cockroaches	3,700	Lurk in dark places. Will eat virtually anything. Often scavenge.
Isoptera	Equal wings	Termites	2,750	Live in huge colonies with one queen who lays all the eggs. Mostly wood-eaters.

Name	Meaning	Examples	Species	Features
Mantodea	Like a prophet	Mantids	2,000	Hunting insects with big eyes and powerful, grasping front legs.
Dermaptera	Leathery wings	Earwigs	1,900	Have pincers at end of abdomen. Fan-shaped rear wings. Will eat anything.
Orthoptera	Straight wings	Crickets, grasshoppers, locusts	20,500	Long back legs for jumping. Eats grass and leaves. May chirp loudly.
Phasmatodea	Like a ghost	Stick insects, leaf insects	2,500	Flat or skinny bodies, well camouflaged to hide on foliage. Eats leaves.
Pscoptera	Milled wings	Book lice, bark lice	3,200	Small, soft-bodied insects that chew tree bark, books, and wrapping.
Phthiraptera	Louse wings	Parasitic lice	6,000	Wingless insects that live on birds and animals. Feed on blood, skin, and feathers.
·Hemiptera	Half wings	True bugs	82,000	Piercing, sucking mouthparts. Feed on plants, insects, or mammals.
Thysanoptera	Fringed wings	Thrips	5,000	Tiny insects that suck plant sap. Can lay eggs without mating.

Megaloptera	Big wings	Alderflies, dobsonflies	300	Larvae are aquatic predators. Adults have long feelers and feed on plants or not at all.
Neuroptera	Net-veined	Lacewings, ant-lions	5,000	Larvae are fierce hunters. Adults are either plant- or meat-eaters.
Coleoptera	Hard wings	Beetles	370,000	Front wings form thick, horny covers for back wings.
Mecoptera	Long wings	Scorpion flies	550	Small hunting insects with biting mouthparts.
Siphonaptera	Tube with no wings	Fleas	2,400	Wingless, but have long hind legs for jumping. Suck the blood of animals.
Diptera	Two wings	Flies	120,000	Adults feed on fresh or rotting plants and animals. Larvae are legless.
Trichoptera	Hairy wings	Caddis flies	10,000	Larvae live in fresh water. Adults feed either on flowers or not at all
Lepidoptera	Scaly wings	Butterflies, moths	165,000	Adults have a long proboscis for drinking nectar. Larvae eat plants.
Hymenoptera	Membrane wings	Ants, bees, wasps	198,000	Mainly meat-eaters, but some prefer plants. Most are solitary, but others live in colonies.

INSECT RECORDS

Heaviest
Goliath beetle – up to 3.5 oz(100 g).

Longest
Indonesian giant stick insect – body 12.9 in (32.8 cm) long. Total length, including legs, of 20 in (50 cm).

Smallest
Mymarid wasps – 0.0067 in (0.17 mm).

Largest wingspan
Australian Hercules moth – 11 in (28 cm) across.

Longest antennae
New Guinea longhorn beetle – 7.5 in (20 cm).

Fastest flier
Some tropical wasps and bees – up to 45 mph (72 kmh).

Fastest wingbeat
The midge *Forcipomyia* – 62,760 beats per minute.

Slowest wingbeat
Swallowtail butterfly – 300 beats per minute.

Fastest runner
Cockroaches of the *Dictyoptera* family – 3.36 mph (5.4 kmh).

Longest jumpers
Desert locust – 19.5 in (50 cm).

Farthest migration
Painted lady butterfly – 4,000 miles (6,436 km), North Africa to Iceland.

Longest lived
Jewel beetles of the *Buprestidae* family – one was known to have lived for at least 47 years.

Shortest lived
Housefly – can complete its entire life cycle in 17 days.

Largest egg
Malaysia's *Heteropteryx dilitata* stick insect – 0.5 in (1.3 cm) long.

Longest time in the egg stage
Titanus giganteus beetle – 9.5 months.

Largest nest
Australian termite – up to 23 ft (7 m) high and 100 ft (31 m) in diameter.

Tallest nest
African termite – up to 42 ft (12.8 m).

Deepest nest
Desert termite – 131 ft (40 m) deep.

Loudest
Some cicadas and mole crickets are audible up to 0.6 miles (1 km) away

Most sensitive sense of smell
Male emperor moth – can detect the scent of a female from almost 7 miles (11 km) away.

Most abundant
Springtails – up to 5,575 per sq ft. (60,000 per sq m).

Insect with the deadliest poison
South African velvet ant (a type of mutillid wasp).

Most murderous
About 40,000 people are killed every year by wasp and bee stings.

Most disease-ridden
The housefly transmits more than 30 diseases and parasites.

Most deadly disease-carriers
Excluding wars and accidents, malaria carried by mosquitoes may have been responsible for 50 percent of human deaths since the Stone Age.

Most destructive
A locust swarm can chomp through 20,000 tons of crops a day.

Most fertile
In theory, with unlimited food and no predators, a cabbage aphid could produce a mass of nymphs weighing 822 million tons in a single year.

BUG GLOSSARY

Abdomen
The rear part of an insect's body, which holds the heart, digestive system, and sexual organs.

Antennae
The two "feelers" on an insect's head that it uses to touch, taste, and smell things. They also detect vibrations.

Arthropod
An animal, such as an insect or a spider, with a jointed body case called an exoskeleton. Arthropods do not have a backbone.

Camouflage
The way animals use shape and color to blend in with their surroundings so that they can hide from view.

Caterpillar
The larval stage of a butterfly or moth after it hatches from an egg.

Chrysalis
A hard protective case surrounding the pupa of an insect, especially a moth or a butterfly.

Cocoon
A silk case spun around a chrysalis.

Colony
A group of ants, wasps, termites, or bees that share the same nest and are all offspring of the same mother – the queen. All the insects in the colony live and work together.

Comb
A series of cells in a bee or wasp nest arranged in rows. Food is stored in the comb and larvae are raised in its cells.

Complete metamorphosis
When an insect has distinct stages of development, from larva to pupa and finally to adult. The larva usually looks very different from the adult,

and often has a different diet.

Compound eye
An insect eye made up of hundreds or even thousands of separate mini-eyes, each containing its own lens and nerve cells.

Courtship
Behavior that leads to the selection of a mate and to mating. In insects, courtship may include making sounds, producing scents, making light, performing dancelike movements, or offering gifts.

Entomologists
Scientists who study insects.

Exoskeleton
The hard, waterproof outer shell of an insect that holds the muscles and body organs in place and gives the insect its shape. It prevents the insect's body from drying out.

Eyespots
Eye-like markings on an insect's body or wings that are used to frighten or startle predators.

Fungus garden
Fungus cultivated in a nest as food by some ants and termites.

Grub
The larval stage in the life of a young beetle, wasp, or bee.

Head
The first of an insect's three body parts. It holds the mouthparts, eyes, antennae, and, of course, the brain.

Habitat
The natural home of a living thing.

Honeydew
The sticky, sweet juice that oozes out of the rear of sap-feeding bugs such as aphids and treehoppers.

Honey guides
Patterns of lines on a flower that guide insects to the flower's nectar.

Incomplete metamorphosis
When an insect develops from a larva to an adult without becoming a pupa. The larva (nymph) looks like a small version of an adult. The larva sheds its skin many times until it reaches adult size.

Larva (plural – larvae)
The first stage of an insect's life after it has hatched from an egg.

Mammal
A warm-blooded animal with a backbone. Mammals drink their mother's milk when they are young.

Mandibles
The main pair of jaws of insects that chew their food. The mandibles have serrated edges. They move from side to side, rather than up and down.

Maxillae
The secondary jaws of chewing insects. Maxillae are mainly used to guide food into the insect's mouth.

Mimic
An insect that copies the looks and often also the behavior of another species in order to gain protection from predators.

Nectar
A sweet liquid produced by flowers. Many insects feed on nectar.

Nymph
Another word for the larval stage of insects that develop by incomplete metamorphosis.

Parasite
An animal that feeds, lives, and grows on or in the body of another animal, called the host.

Pollen
Dustlike plant particles that contain the male sex cells of a flower. Pollen must be carried between flowers in order for fruit, nuts, or seeds to form.

Pollination
The transfer of pollen from the male part of one flower to the female part (ovary) of another flower. Plants are pollinated by insects, bats, birds, and even by the wind.

Predator
An animal that kills other animals, known as prey, for food.

Proboscis
The tubelike mouthparts of some insects that have liquid diets.

Prolegs
Muscular projections from the body of a caterpillar that help it to grip surfaces such as leaves and twigs.

Pupa (plural – pupae)
This is the resting stage of an insect that undergoes complete metamorphosis, during which it develops from a larva into an adult by a complete body change.

Queen
The founder and sole egg-laying female of a colony of ants, bees, wasps, or termites.

Saliva
A liquid secreted in the mouth that begins the process of digesting food.

Sap
A liquid that transports nutrients in plants. Many insects feed on sap.

Sense hairs
Tiny hairs on an insect's body that can detect smells, tastes, sounds, and vibrations. Each sense hair is connected to a nerve.

Simple eyes
The primitive eyes of insect larvae and some adults. They can only detect differences in light and shade.

Social insects
Those insects that live together in colonies. Ants, wasps, bees, and termites are all social insects.
Soldiers
Insects in a colony whose sole task is to defend the nest against intruders. Soldier insects cannot breed.
Species
A group of animals with similar features that can breed with one another to produce fertile young.
Spiracles
Tiny holes along an insect's body through which it breathes.
Sting
The sharp body part of some bees, wasps, or ants that is used to inject poison into prey or attackers.
Territory
An area where an insect lives and which it will defend against intruders.
Thorax
The middle part of an insect's body, to which the legs and wings attach. The thorax holds muscles for moving the legs and wings.
Ultraviolet light
Part of normal daylight that is beyond the range of human vision, but which insects can see.
Wing cases
The protective coverings of a beetle's rear wings. Wing cases are formed from the front wings, which are no longer needed for flight.
Worker
A member of an insect colony whose duties include caring for the larvae, foraging for food, and maintaining the nest. Like soldiers, workers are sterile and cannot breed.

BUG WEBSITES

www.yahooligans.com/Science_and_Nature/Living_Things/Animals/Invertebrates/Arthropods/Insects/
This excellent site lists dozens of other insect websites that are updated and checked by the editors of Yahooligans – that's the kids' section of Yahoo.
http://yucky.kids.discovery.com/
Check out the gory cockroach stuff at this Discovery Channel site. There's plenty of other yucky stuff too.
www.wnet.org/nature/alienempire/
From PBS TV, this insect site has video clips and interactive presentations.
www.pbs.org/wgbh/nova/bees/
A website about a movie made inside a beehive. Find out how the movie was made, and get a bee's-eye view of how a hive works.
www.eatbug.com/
This site is all about eating bugs, complete with recipes!
www.mesc.usgs.gov/butterfly/butterfly.html
A children's butterfly site run by the US Geological Survey.
http://ant.edb.miyakyo-u.ac.jp/INTRODUCTION/Gakken79E/title.html
A Japanese photo-encyclopedia of ants with lots of in-depth information.

INDEX

CREDITS

Dorling Kindersley would like to thank:
Nomazwe Madonko and Almudena Diaz for DTP assistance; Kate Humby for proofreading; and Chris Bernstein for compiling the index.

Additional photography by:
Jane Burton, Neil Fletcher, Frank Greenaway, Colin Keates, Dave King, Kim Taylor
Thanks also to model makers Roby Baum, Jonathan Hateley, Gary Staab